I Want to Teach

my CHiLD About

Media

BY

KIRSETIN MORELLO

Standard®
PUBLISHING
Bringing The Word to Life

Cincinnati, Ohio

Produced by Susan Lingo Books™
Cover and interior by Diana Walters

12 11 10 09 08 07 06 05   9 8 7 6 5 4 3 2
0-7847-1769-9

Contents

Introduction

Why teach your child about media?

Books and studies warn us about the dangers of television and the Internet. Most parents have heard about violent video games and seen suggestive sexual dancing on MTV or innuendo on prime-time television shows. But how does it affect our kids? How much of what we hear is hype? As parents, we certainly have cause for concern, but this isn't a book for the alarmist. You won't find suggestions to boycott your local movie theater or unplug your cable cord. What you will find in these pages is lots of practical information and tips on positive ways your kids can use media, including computers, the Internet, television, music, movies, newspapers, and video games. You'll also discover tips for teaching your kids how to be discerning media consumers, because, at some point, they'll be making media decisions on their own.

Until that time, it can be hard to know where to draw the line. It's tough to reject the argument: "But everyone's going to the movie, Mom," when our response is based solely on a gut reaction. It's much easier when we've established family values and viewing guidelines to guide our decisions. This book will help you and your kids think through and articulate the values that represent your family's beliefs. Our children are "fearfully and wonderfully made" (Psalm 139:14) by our Heavenly Father. As their earthly parents, it's our job to integrate them into the real world slowly, to nurture and teach them about the joys and dangers they'll face, and to provide them with protective armor. It's my hope that this book will help.

Kirsetin Karamarkovich Morello

Where Do You Stand?

Working toward helping your child learn about media and how it affects his life is an important part of parenting. The following questionnaire will help you evaluate your own strengths and weaknesses and where your own values and philosophies fit in. Circle the number that best corresponds to your answer.

OPTIONS

❶ Strongly agree

❷ Agree somewhat

❸ Disagree somewhat

❹ Strongly disagree

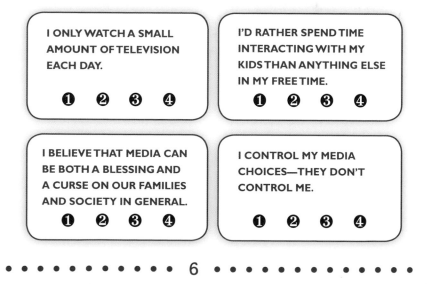

I ONLY WATCH A SMALL AMOUNT OF TELEVISION EACH DAY.

❶   ❷   ❸   ❹

I'D RATHER SPEND TIME INTERACTING WITH MY KIDS THAN ANYTHING ELSE IN MY FREE TIME.

❶   ❷   ❸   ❹

I BELIEVE THAT MEDIA CAN BE BOTH A BLESSING AND A CURSE ON OUR FAMILIES AND SOCIETY IN GENERAL.

❶   ❷   ❸   ❹

I CONTROL MY MEDIA CHOICES—THEY DON'T CONTROL ME.

❶   ❷   ❸   ❹

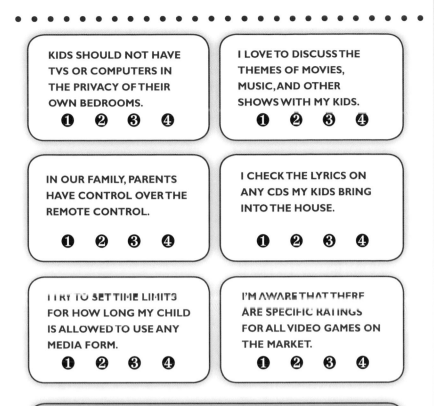

KIDS SHOULD NOT HAVE TVS OR COMPUTERS IN THE PRIVACY OF THEIR OWN BEDROOMS.
❶ ❷ ❸ ❹

I LOVE TO DISCUSS THE THEMES OF MOVIES, MUSIC, AND OTHER SHOWS WITH MY KIDS.
❶ ❷ ❸ ❹

IN OUR FAMILY, PARENTS HAVE CONTROL OVER THE REMOTE CONTROL.
❶ ❷ ❸ ❹

I CHECK THE LYRICS ON ANY CDS MY KIDS BRING INTO THE HOUSE.
❶ ❷ ❸ ❹

I TRY TO SET TIME LIMITS FOR HOW LONG MY CHILD IS ALLOWED TO USE ANY MEDIA FORM.
❶ ❷ ❸ ❹

I'M AWARE THAT THERE ARE SPECIFIC RATINGS FOR ALL VIDEO GAMES ON THE MARKET.
❶ ❷ ❸ ❹

HOW YOU SCORED

10—20 You're a media master! You realize that if we're not careful with our time, media can control us instead of the other way around. In a world saturated by media and media hype, you understand the importance of guiding your child's choices and using veto power when necessary. Keep it up!

21—31 You enjoy using media—maybe a bit too much! You probably prefer to use media only in your spare time, but you may not be as diligent about limiting your kids' time in front of the "tube" or computer. Stay on guard in helping your kids recognize the pleasures—and dangers—of media.

32—40 Media just may have a hold on you! Though you may feel guilty for spending a bit too much time shopping online or watching just one more TV show, you find it hard to push the stop button on your electronic "toys." You may need to look at curbing your own media use to provide a good role model for your kids. Media is fun—but in controlled doses.

Media and Its Uses

Children today face more media choices than ever. In fact, most American kids spend six hours of every day in front of a computer, video, or television screen. Even if that number seems shocking, we can't deny that television, music, video games, books, magazines, and the Internet are an integral part of the lives we live.

Media surrounds our lives every day.

Have you ever wondered about the impact media is having on your kids? It's hard not to wonder in a time when the average family has two televisions, two VCRs, two CD players, one video-game player, and a computer, too! As parents, it's our job to guide, supervise, and teach our children how to harness the power of media to their advantage and to avoid the murky waters that surround it.

key point
MEDIA INFLUENCES KIDS.

Media is a powerful force.

Media is undeniably influential. Our kids watch the nightly news and see world events as they happen, they use the Internet to learn about scientific discoveries around the world, and they read books and magazines for education and enjoyment. But we need to guard against media's negative influences as well. Childhood obesity, tobacco and alcohol use, distorted body image, sexual promiscuity, and poor academic achievement all have links to excessive or inappropriate use of the media.

TARGET MOMENT

When your child encounters inappropriate material, you face a choice: ignore it or confront it. Choose to confront it! Use this time to compare and contrast your family's beliefs with the values portrayed by the media.

key point
MEDIA REQUIRES CAREFUL CHOICES.

Three of these negative influences—obesity, body image, and poor academic achievement—affect kids as early as elementary school. Simply watching music videos or surfing the Internet isn't the culprit. Trouble develops when use becomes extreme or our children make poor choices. By helping kids develop "media literacy," ascertaining both the message and who's behind it, we help kids use media wisely.

When kids stop and examine media, they need to use critical thinking and discernment. Rather than taking these messages at face value, encourage your child to stop and wonder about who's behind any hidden meanings and to ask: "Do I agree with this message?"

Make a family media plan for the coming week. Choose which programs, video games, music, magazines, and Internet sites you'll enjoy. Then use media only when it's scheduled and stick to the schedule!

Helping our kids interpret, comprehend, and scrutinize media is only half of the battle. The other half is setting boundaries. Rules for media choices need to be in line with the values that characterize your family. And remember: What we read, watch, and listen to ourselves send powerful messages to our kids about the authenticity of our values!

Percent of American homes with a TV

Media is here to stay.

So how do we deal with the impact of such varied influences? First we need to realize that content matters. While books, television, and the Internet teach our children many things, they can also be incredibly influential in shaping ideas, trends, and standards that are not based on biblical teachings. To counteract such influences, we need to guide our children to use media productively and creatively and to teach them to evaluate all they see, read, and hear.

key point
CONTENT COUNTS!

key point
RECOGNIZE MEDIA'S INFLUENCE.

We enjoy and share experiences with our children by watching movies or television shows, reading books aloud, or listening to the radio. It's precisely because our kids will spend a lot of time with media, and much of it alone, that we must teach them to be careful critics.

A good place to start is thinking about what your child likes. If dinosaurs fascinate your four-year-old, check out dinosaur books and explore Internet sites with dinosaur games and facts. When your fourteen-year-old announces she's a vegetarian, go online together to look up new recipes. As your kids get older, you can discuss the themes in movies, books, and magazine articles as a family.

TIPS FOR TODDLERS

Read books to your infant. Try *Goodnight Moon* **by Margaret Wise Brown (Harper-Festival).**

For CDs, try "Baby Beluga" by Raffi (Rounder/Pgd Media).

Share lively, educational software with preschoolers. Try Reader Rabbit Pre-School (The Learning Company).

Another positive way we use media is to encourage our kid's creativity. Does your child love word searches? Head to www. kidsdomain.com and print off loads of word-search fun. Craft books abound with hours of creative ideas. Or try a family movie night, and choose movies that spark interesting family discussions. *Talking Pictures* by Ronald Madison and Corey Schmidt provides lists of movies that deal with topics such as friendship, prejudice, and family life.

key point
USE MEDIA WISELY—NOT LIBERALLY!

TRY THIS!

Go to www.google.com or www.yahoo.com and enter phrases such as "free coloring" or "games for kids." You'll be led you to sites filled with cool games and puzzles. Try searching for "planets," "kids activities," or "coin collecting" for even more fun!

Log on to the Internet with your child and check out these sites together.

Ages 3-5
www.coloring.ws

Ages 6-8
www.familyfun.go.com

Ages 9-12
www.funology.com

Ages 10+
www.nationalgeographic.com/kids

MEDIA SURROUNDS OUR LIVES EVERY DAY.

Visual input sways our memories.

Kids today have unprecedented access to the arts, world politics, and remote cultures. Ultimately, media offers our kids access to people, places, events, and information that might otherwise be unavailable.

Media brings the world up close and personal.

With two televisions in most homes, TV broadcasts are a particularly effective way to see events from around the globe. Visual images make powerful impressions! For example, watching the Olympics provides time to discuss the merits of hard work and achieving goals through patience and perseverance as we "run the good race."

When we watch sports, we must also be ready to discuss sportsmanship, privilege, and responsibility. When kids see players throw tantrums or hit another athlete, it gives us a chance to discuss the incident and what Jesus might have done. Use opportunities like this to discuss how media and values—or the lack thereof—influence decisions.

DON'T FORGET

Remind kids that the Bible is God's infallible Word that provides us with clear guidelines for right and wrong— even in the world of sports! When we live and act by God's principles for right and wrong, there are no gray areas!

Seeing TV "heroes" or "hooligans" in action is only one way visual imagery affects kids. Access to art is one area that's often overlooked. Online, we can share the paintings of Claude Monet with young children from the comfort of our own home, then buy finger-paints to let our kids create their own masterpieces. Older kids may learn about artists from Michelangelo to Andy Warhol. When kids develop an appreciation for art, it provides them with a broader base of knowledge from which to make judgments and decisions.

key point
MEDIA CAN PROMOTE UNDERSTANDING.

key point
INFORMATION IS EVERYWHERE!

BIG BIBLE POINT

Proper use of media combined with biblical principles can help our kids develop empathy, compassion, and forgiveness, the very qualities God wants us to develop. Read Ephesians 4:32 with your kids, then discuss how knowing God's Word and how He desires us to behave helps us choose what to watch or how to respond to what we see on TV.

Perhaps one of the biggest advantages of media access is that our kids have the opportunity to investigate other cultures. The impact of visual images from poverty-stricken areas, homes destroyed by fire or flood, or grief-stricken parents can encourage our children to develop empathy for others. Likewise, when kids see images of magnificent scenes or beautiful families of all sizes, shapes, and colors, it can produce a vast appreciation for all of God's creation. Reading, watching, and listening to diverse stories about other areas can help reveal, and close, the cultural gaps within our communities.

When our kids begin to understand the people of other cultures, it promotes empathy and compassion.

VISUAL INPUT SWAYS OUR MEMORIES.

Media creates images in our hearts and minds.

Much of the media we use today is visual. The images we see create powerful thoughts and feelings in our hearts and minds. When kids read or listen to words, their minds create images that then exist in the database of their memories. The danger comes with seeing repeated negative images over time—we begin to believe them.

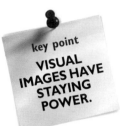

key point
VISUAL IMAGES HAVE STAYING POWER.

A prime example of this power is in media's illustration of the rail-thin figures of models and actresses. Years of media images have made many now accept rail-thin physiques as normal. Young girls especially strive to achieve these emaciated figures because they have come to believe what they see in magazines, TV shows, and movies.

In an era when people can contract the deadly HIV virus from one sexual mishap, the media has essentially looked the other way. Unmarried couples in movies, television shows, magazines, advertisements, and music videos frequently have sex and face no consequences. Sexually transmitted diseases, teen pregnancies, and feelings of worthlessness that result are rarely addressed.

What are your TV habits? Track what and when you watch for one week, then evaluate your habits and be ready to make changes if necessary!

TIPS FOR 'TWEENS

Create a "top ten" poster of your family's values such as honesty, forgiveness, or modesty. Display the poster by your TV. If a show breaks one or more of the "top ten," choose different programming!

key point

BE DILIGENT AND VIGILANT WITH MEDIA!

The power of the media is clear: the images we see leave imprints on our minds and hearts. While we can't control every image our kids see or hear on the media, we can establish guidelines to foster good practices. Encourage kids to compare what they see and hear by what God teaches. The more positive images our children record, the easier it will be for them to "make level paths for [their] feet and take only ways that are firm," as it teaches us to do in Proverbs 4:26.

Approximately 8 of 10 teen girls are unhappy with their bodies.

Audio input is greatly influential.

It's not just what we see that matters—what we hear has a powerful influence, too! When we direct our kids toward positive uses of audio media, the outcome can be beneficial instead of worrisome.

Media helps people express themselves.

key point
MUSIC COMMUNICATES FEELINGS.

key point
MUSIC CAN LIFT KIDS OR PULL THEM DOWN!

Artists differ vastly in their approaches to producing music, which means that some create constructive music while others pound out destructive noise. We want to be certain our kids choose musical artists who create music with positive, upbeat messages.

Ever notice how toddlers love to dance in time to lively rhythms? Even teens appreciate instrumentals, although we shouldn't expect them to trade all of the tunes on their MP3 players for jazz or blues. Exposing our kids to instrumental music helps broaden their horizons and provides yet another opportunity to connect as a family through this lively source of media.

TRY THIS!

Enjoy a fun family activity that includes everyone by creating your own expressive movie. 'Tweens can write a short script, and other family members can make props. Encourage everyone to express himself in creative ways as you film your "masterpiece"!

TIPS FOR TODDLERS

Invite your toddler to express himself by painting, drawing, or gluing craft scraps to paper plates as he listens to lively music. For more media fun, check out special events or rhythm classes for very young children through community or church programs.

Precisely because music has the power to move us, it's also a terrific outlet for children to express themselves. Whether your daughter is interested in piano, drum, or voice lessons isn't relevant. Our goal as parents isn't to produce concert pianists or famous singers but to encourage kids to pursue musical interests. Musical outlets allow children the freedom to express themselves in positive ways rather than pursuing more harmful pastimes or habits.

PARENTS POINTER

How we think affects our moods and actions and colors almost everything in our lives. Remind kids that what we think in our hearts makes us who we are and that media choices affect how we express ourselves in positive or negative ways.

How we facilitate our kids' musical appreciation depends in part on their ages and interests. Toddlers enjoy programs and videos containing lively music and movement. If your child shows interest in a specific musical instrument, consider music lessons by first or second grade.

AUDIO INPUT IS GREATLY INFLUENTIAL.

Media affects us all in different ways.

Hearing or playing the same piece of music affects each of us differently. Seeing the same news story creates unique feelings as well. What makes one person smile may cause another to cry. But though media affects us in different ways, one thing is true—it has a lasting effect!

key point
EXPERIENCES MAKE US INDIVIDUALS.

Because we interpret music differently, there's no clear-cut answer to what makes some children react more strongly to negative lyrics than others. There is a noticeable difference in our kids when they listen to positive music that evokes feelings of peace and joy than when they listen to negative imagery and sounds. Remind your child that true joy and peace—which is what you desire for her—comes from a righteous heart that loves God.

TARGET MOMENT

Use the pause button on your VCR or TiVo to talk to your kids about how music influences the mood of the TV show or movie you're watching. Ask kids:
• How does music contribute to the emotion of the scene?
• How does the music make you feel?
• Rewind and play the scene without sound. How does this change the mood?

Music has another interesting effect on our kids. It can stimulate their minds. Scientists have wondered about the effect for years, and some studies show a link between a child's exposure to classical music and improved spatial and reasoning skills. In addition, the College Board's annual analysis of national SAT scores shows that kids who have had experience with musical study score better on both the verbal and math sections of the SAT!

PARENTS POINTER

Media has the power to encourage or discourage. Help your kids realize that a commercial for toothpaste may promise you whiter teeth, but it may not deliver on the promise. Remind your kids that all media needs to be thought of as the foods we eat. Just as we become what we eat, we may become our media choices! Don't be fooled!

Help your child understand the connection between music and emotions. The next time you hear suspenseful music or sound effects in a movie, point it out. Ask if the scene would be as tense without the audio track. This helps kids develop a critical ear about the music they like and the influences it has on them.

key point
MEDIA CREATES EXPERIENCES.

Remember:
"Man becomes what he thinks about all day long."
—Ralph W. Emerson
Choose media carefully!

Media can have entertainment value.

At one time or another, most of us have taken a break from our day with a good book, a funny movie, or by surfing the Internet. Whatever source we choose, media has the ability to make us laugh, cry, and pass the time.

Used in healthy doses, media can relax us.

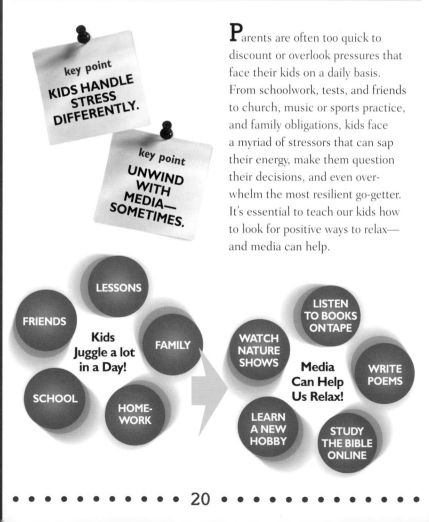

Parents are often too quick to discount or overlook pressures that face their kids on a daily basis. From schoolwork, tests, and friends to church, music or sports practice, and family obligations, kids face a myriad of stressors that can sap their energy, make them question their decisions, and even overwhelm the most resilient go-getter. It's essential to teach our kids how to look for positive ways to relax—and media can help.

Like adults, children handle stress differently. Some kids manage school projects, sports, and family activities with ease, while others do not. Whether your child balances many balls or prefers to take things at a slower pace, she needs time to relax. In their fast-paced lives, it can be hard for our children to recognize when they need to slow down. It's our job to teach them, and for many of us media is part of the equation. Whether we encourage our kids to curl up with a new book or laugh at the latest sitcom, sensible use of media can give our kids a respite from their hectic lives.

BIG BIBLE POINT

Share Psalm 101:2 with your child and then discuss these questions:

• What kinds of shows or movies do you enjoy watching together?

• What are your favorite books, or do you read at all?

• How long do you spend relaxing with your media choices?

• Do your choices honor God or offend Him?

• How can you relax with media and still grow closer to God?

For relaxing, fun writing and reading, check out these print magazines that publish the work of kids.

Potluck (www.members.aol. com/potluckmagazine)

Young Writer (www.myst-world.com/youngwriter)

Creative Kids (www.prufrock.com)

A new "how-to" book can provide kids interested in photography with hours of pleasurable and relaxing entertainment. Other kids might be interested in becoming an author or film producer. Online sites like www. cyberkids.com/cw (for the budding author) and www.listenup.org (for the film buff) can help in these pursuits. Help your child learn how to relax with media while she hones a skill or learns a new hobby.

Media can unleash imagination and creativity.

There are a number of ways kids can use media to develop their imaginations and creativity. Through creativity, kids learn to cope with the challenges of childhood, solve problems, and deal with difficult situations or changes in their lives. Imaginative children realize that there may not always be just one right answer to a problem. The merits of encouraging creativity in our kids are clear, but how can media help?

key point
CREATIVITY HELPS KIDS SOLVE PROBLEMS.

Fortunately, there are lots of ways to engage our kids' imaginations! We can start with babies while we look at picture books. When we ask our preschoolers what they see in pictures, they learn to express ideas. Older kids read more elaborate stories, and we can talk to them about how they would handle different scenarios that may one day help them with solutions to real-life problems.

key point
MEDIA STIMULATES CREATIVITY.

There are a number of computer programs that allow kids to "paint," draw, or compose music. Older kids can use computer software to crop digital photos for a family project. Kids learn a lot about themselves as they explore the creative process through media!

Go on a media safari and capture everyone's creativity! Work as a family to complete these creative activities from different media sources.

- **Illustrate a poem from a BOOK of poetry.**
- **Paint an impression of music from a SONG.**
- **Look up "ibex" ONLINE, then write a rhyme about an ibex.**
- **Create a favorite foods collage from MAGAZINE pictures.**

Music also allows kids to cut loose and exercise their creative talents. Children love instruments, whether they're purchased at a store or made from cardboard and craft bells. While teens may eschew homemade instruments, they can take lessons, compose, record, and perform their own songs. If your child is interested, there are several CD-ROMs, like "Making More Music," and online resources to help them explore more about music on their own.

TIPS FOR TODDLERS

High-tech, computerized media is fun, but don't forget to provide "old-fashioned" activities such as finger painting, coloring, playing music with spoons and pot lids, or searching for "treasures" in your home or yard.

Media is a powerful information system.

Media is an omnipresent force in kids' young lives. In order for them to make wise decisions about what they hear, we must teach them to evaluate the messages and discern the truth.

News travels faster than it can be verified.

key point
MEDIA IMAGES CAN BE ALTERED.

Try some fun with a digital camera to see how easy it is to modify photos. Take a digital photo or scan a picture into your computer or into a photo machine at a retail store. Crop and retouch the photo to see how easy it is to change reality. Print the original and "new" photos and compare them.

We often see or hear about current events as they happen, and if our kids are watching, they see it, too. Television cameras are in courtrooms and war zones. Political events and news stories are broadcast live. Because of this potential, filtering news coverage has to be an integral part of guarding our children's hearts.

The speed with which newsrooms *can* report a story has led to a new quandary: How quickly *should* they report? In the 2000 presidential election, late in the evening Pacific Standard Time, the TV news stations reported that George W. Bush had won the electoral votes for the state of Florida and called the election in his favor. In reality, it would be weeks before a final determination was made. Talking to our kids about events like this illustrates that checking facts has always been important—and is *vital* today.

TARGET MOMENT

Go to www.google.com and type in the name of a person you know or admire. Compare what you know to be true about this person with what you read on the Internet. If another person with the same name pops up, talk about the importance of accuracy and fact checking.

Digital photography and the Internet also play roles in the accuracy of the news we receive. What that means for our children is that a picture might really be worth a thousand fibs. Even a 'tweenager can create an authentic-looking Web site filled with inaccurate and biased "news."

With all the possibilities and factors influencing the news, should we simply teach our kids to disregard it all? Of course not! What we need to teach them is vigilance and discernment. Kids need to measure news reports by what they already know to be true and by the values they believe in. In this era of rapid reporting, kids need to research the facts and the people behind the stories.

"Television news is like a lightning flash. It makes a loud noise, lights up everything around it, leaves everything else in darkness and then is suddenly gone."
—Hodding Carter

key point
NEWS ACCURACY ISN'T A GIVEN.

Media creates a melting pot of information.

The influence of popular culture is formidable and arrives into our children's world through the characters and themes of movies, television, print media, and music, as well as through the actions of actors and artists themselves. Books, magazines, Internet sites, and news reports impact perceptions of reality until there's a melting pot of information assailing our kids daily!

key point
INFORMATION MUST BE SIFTED THROUGH.

key point
MEDIA CAN SEND MIXED MESSAGES.

COFFEE BREAK

- What information shows does your child listen to?
- Who or what group is behind these messages?
- Is the information your child hears biased?
- How can you help provide a more rounded view?

Because a dichotomy often exists between the messages our kids receive from their inner circle of friends and family and from the world at large, they are left to sort through a mishmash of contradictory information. A prime example of this inconsistency is the mixed messages about cigarette smoking. Media tells kids it's unhealthy, yet many Hollywood stars are filmed smoking. But this isn't the only area with mixed messages. Consider what kids' favorite CDs or TV shows tell them about love, alcohol, sex, and drugs.

Despite warnings from the American Academy of Pediatrics, many kids have TV sets in their bedrooms. Remember: You can't monitor the content, and your kids may choose to omit family interaction time with a TV set in their bedrooms!

56%

46%

20%

12- to 17-year-olds   8- to 12-year-olds   2 to 7 year-olds

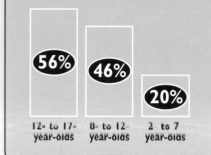

TIPS FOR 'TWEENS

Kids need to understand the context of the opinions they hear and read. For example, politicians may use the same statistics to debate opposite sides of an issue. Discuss differing opinions, then have kids summarize the debate in one sentence.

Another area that influences our children's developing opinions is found in the newsroom. Ideally, news informs us and presents an unbiased, truthful reporting of events. Unfortunately, the truth is often distorted and presented as fact. We should pray that, like Daniel, God will give our children "insight, intelligence and outstanding wisdom" (Daniel 5:14) so they are better able to make wise decisions regarding what they believe.

How can parents help kids navigate the varying information and opinions they encounter from media? Watch and listen alongside children! When we take time to share media experiences, we're better able to discuss, inform, and guide kids with discerning choices through this enormous melting pot of information!

Media can be an effective teaching tool.

Media can entertain us and inform us, yes, but don't overlook its potential for educating. With the Internet, magazines, books, and movies all readily available we can take advantage of learning opportunities even when we're not at school.

Media can offer solid teaching strategies.

We teach our kids to mind their manners and how to tie their shoes. We teach them patience and mercy. And whether we teach them to read and write as well, the most important lesson they learn from us is to live lives that honor God. It might seem that media doesn't have a place here, but because biblical values and morals aren't the only things we teach our children, it's anything but irrelevant!

key point
THERE ARE DIFFERENT LEARNING STYLES.

When our children are toddlers and preschoolers, we have a unique chance to be with them when there's nowhere else they'd rather be. It's during this stage that our children's personalities begin to emerge. We realize that some like puzzles, some like being read to, and some prefer running endlessly. These early inclinations have a direct correlation to our children's ideal *learning styles*.

key point
MEDIA CAN BE EDUCATIONAL.

L̲earning styles? Even if you're unfamiliar with the term, it's quite likely that you already know what it means. Many parents are aware that children, even within the same family, learn differently. Kids who love puzzles most likely learn by seeing and are *visual learners.* Kids who could listen to stories all day are *auditory learners,* and kids who learn best when actively doing and touching are *tactile* or *kinesthetic learners.*

C̲hoose and use a variety of media sources to stimulate a variety of learning styles! Educational TV shows are great for visual and auditory learners. Educational Web sites offer fun for hands-on learners, and software that creates art or music stimulates all learning styles. Guide your child to try a variety of media outlets to stimulate imagination and learning.

VISUAL LEARNERS

• Subscribe to lively, visual kid's magazines such as *Ladybug* and *Spider* (Cobblestone Publishing Company).
• Consider computer software that allows kids to create art, cartoons, or cool charts and presentations.
• For sites that are entertaining *and* educational, try www.si.edu/kids or www.pbskids.org/zoom.

AUDITORY LEARNERS

• Look into the software program *Alice in Vivaldi's Four Seasons* to help kids learn about music and musical instruments by playing musical puzzles and games.
• Check the library for audio CDs or books on cassette tapes.

KINESTHETIC LEARNERS

• Log on to Web sites that provide hands-on activities to try at home. Try www.hhmi.org/coolscience or www.funology.com.
• Check out CDs such as *Can Cockatoos Count by Twos?* by Hap Palmer (Hap-Pal Music) that combine learning, music, and movement for young children.
• For older kids, peruse the many wonderful ideas for combining physical activities and learning fun at www.pecentral.org.

MEDIA CAN BE AN EFFECTIVE TEACHING TOOL.

Media can educate families.

PARENTS POINTER

Books and the Internet are great tools for researching volunteer opportunities to do together. Deciding on a volunteer project serves two purposes: it increases the amount of time you spend together as a family, and it teaches your children the value of giving generously and without grudging hearts. (Deuteronomy 15:10)

Family time has become an endangered species in many homes. We're busy with so many good things, including work, volunteering, church activities, and carting kids. We can use media to help provide educational and enrichment opportunities that draw us closer together as families.

Part of the fabric that holds families together is a sense of unity. The activities you do are less important than setting aside the time to share them, and media can play an inviting role in drawing you closer. Perusing books and exploring the Internet can help you discover new interests. By using various forms of media, you can be sure to keep things interesting.

TRY THIS!

Use the Internet to plan virtual or real trips. For example, take the family on a virtual trip to Yellowstone National Park using the Internet to decide how to get there and what to do during your visit. Check out the library for more books to help with planning trips.

Sit down as a family and choose one night a week for spending time together. Choose activities everyone can participate in, like reading books aloud or working on a family scrapbook. If you watch a TV show or movie, you can chat about what you watched over a bowl of popcorn afterwards.

Designate a jar as the Media Jar. Write forms of media on slips of paper, including movies, TV, CDs, books, computer, and Internet. Each week pull a paper out of the jar. If you choose "computer," play lively spelling or geography games on your PC or Mac. If you choose "books," dig out your recipe books and make a new recipe to share. Look for all the exciting ways media can educate your family as it increases communication, cooperation, and togetherness.

key point
FAMILY TIME IS ESSENTIAL.

key point
MEDIA CAN DRAW FAMILIES CLOSER.

TARGET MOMENT

Not time for a trip to the zoo? Log on to zoo sites around the world for a virtual visit! Have your child type "zoo" into a search engine, then begin your safari. Keep a notebook of which zoos you visit and list your favorite animals from each. You may even be able to print off pictures of your favorites! Whether you're virtually visiting zoos, planetariums, or farms, it will be a learning experience the whole family can enjoy!

Media and Its Forms

We know that different types of media are more effective for different learning styles and that each form of media has its own benefits and drawbacks. By appreciating these differences, we can guide our kids toward safe and effective use of all media types.

Words in print pack a punch!

When we hear about media literacy, we often think of computers and television, but the old standard—the printed word—is extremely powerful! To understand the power of the written word, consider the impact the Bible has had on lives and cultures around the world.

Books have the power to change lives.

key point
READING PROMOTES EMPATHY.

Children who read learn language, comprehension skills, and new ideas faster and consistently perform better in school than children who don't have this advantage. Early reading lays the groundwork for a lifelong appreciation of reading, so that when our children get their first "big-kid Bible," they'll be both able and excited to read it.

Although we may disagree with some of what is written, books and magazines do have the power to challenge kids to think critically. The written word introduces kids to a wide range of cultures and perspectives that promote empathy and understanding.

There are wonderful Christian resources in print! Choose classic books such as *The Chronicles of Narnia* or hop into more "hip" books for preteens, including *Can I Be a Christian Without Being Weird?* (Bethany House Publishers). Books help kids draw conclusions about the world around them and can offer life-changing views.

key point
THERE'S POWER IN THE WRITTEN WORD.

Consider subscribing to a magazine your child might enjoy. Kids love the thrill and anticipation of awaiting each issue in the mail. Then when it arrives, set aside time to share the magazine—and some fun—with your child!

TIPS FOR 'TWEENS

Get your 'tween started with these wholesome, classic books:

- *The Secret Garden* by Frances Hodgson Burnett
- *The Diary of a Young Girl* by Anne Frank
- The "Little House" Series by Laura Ingalls Wilder
- *Christy* by Catherine Marshall

Reading requires thought and discernment.

70%–80% of the people in the U.S. read newspapers and magazines monthly.

With all of the advantages of reading, what do parents have to worry about? Content and bias! What messages is my child reading? Are they healthy or destructive ones? Bias means that what people write is influenced by their life experiences, convictions, and backgrounds. We must teach our kids to discern the facts from the agenda in messages!

Pick up a copy of two news magazines on opposite sides of the political spectrum. Find articles that deal with the same facts, such as a recent election or an ongoing war. With your older child, compare and contrast the differences in the attitudes, tones, and suggestions. Talk about how writers use the same facts but draw different conclusions. These are the analytical skills your child needs to evaluate media.

DON'T FORGET

Help your child to remember that a person or someone representing a school of thought is behind everything he reads— and it requires careful thought to decide if we'll believe what we read!

Even within the realm of Christianity, our kids will eventually face discord. Disagreement over issues can lead to intense conflict and cause churches to divide. The ability to read and comprehend the Bible, as well as the works of other Christians, helps your child understand and apply what he believes and enables him to take a stand on important issues.

key point
WRITERS' BIASES SPILL INTO THEIR WORK.

BIG BIBLE POINT

"My son, preserve sound judgment and discernment, do not let them out of your sight" (Proverbs 3:21). **Share this verse aloud with your child, then ask:**
- **Why is it good to think about what we read?**
- **How can words sway our thinking, either positively or negatively?**
- **Is it okay to disagree with what you read? Explain.**

key point
WRITTEN MEDIA STIRS THOUGHT.

Our children will eventually come to understand that not everyone in the world, our country, or even our own communities has the same religious beliefs. There will be times when kids read opinions that directly contradict what they've learned at home and in church. The time kids spend contemplating these differences with discernment will only strengthen and develop their faith. As a parent, you can help your child build a strong foundation in his critical-reading skills and in thinking about what is being read and communicated. We need to *inform* our kids about these differences, *teach* them to read with a critical and analytical eye, and encourage them to *discuss* the ideas they read!

It's important to be good film critics.

Who doesn't love a good movie? But tastes change as we get older and better at seeing the whole picture and as we're able to separate fact, fiction, and fantasy!

Film can create fantasy or cement reality.

Film is an influential venue for screenwriters, directors, producers, and actors to convey agendas. Our children need to be aware that these are ordinary people doing a rather extraordinary job. It doesn't mean their ideas are better or their values more worthy. Once kids understand this, they become film critics who enjoy a story without buying into any propaganda it might contain.

Another reason we need to be good film critics is that the grown-up world portrayed in the movies isn't anything like the grown-up world most of us live in. Reality is full of intricacies that movies don't—or can't possibly—capture. It's extremely important for kids to understand that actors on the big screen are merely doing their jobs and that many stories are not reality; they're only echoes of realism.

Do you measure yourself by the Hollywood benchmark of "beauty" and "fast" living? We must lead by example and allow our children to see us experience true contentment from God's hand—not from distorted images of someone else's reality!

Help kids separate fact from fantasy in what they watch.

IT'S A PROBLEM OF PERCEPTION!

9- to 10-year-olds	13-year-olds	17-year-olds
40%	53%	78%

Many young girls are unhappy with their bodies when compared to the images they see in the media. What messages are our kids getting as they grow older?
USA Today (1996)

Some movies promote unrealistic ideals through the physical attributes of the stars. Our daughters see thin, beautiful women, and our sons see strong, attractive men. They don't see the eating disorders, tortured self-images, and plastic surgery that often accompany the pretty pictures on the screen. Even kids as young as nine or ten are negatively affected when they compare themselves to movie-star standards.

key point
MOVIES CAN DISTORT REALITY.

To offset these influences, encourage your child to watch more realistic movies that depict current social issues and capture how kids feel about them. Viewing these movies together can open up entire lines of realistic communication that we may never have considered and give us a glimpse into a different window of our children's lives.

BIG BIBLE POINT

Read Philippians 4:11-13 with your child and ask him to think about his own reality and what makes him pleased and contented. TV shows often try to force someone else's vision of happiness onto the audience. Remind your child that God made him wonderful and gives him many blessings that make his reality one to be treasured!

Movie actors are just people—for better or worse!

Until our kids really grasp the concept that actors are imperfect people doing a job, we must guide them through the process. A good place to start is with Exodus 34:14, which says: "Do not worship any other god...." It's easy for kids to idolize the glamorous people they see on the screen. It's our job to ground them in reality to avoid the tribulations that come with displacing God.

Let your 'tween do the research on charities that a few of her favorite stars support. She should learn about the charity, including its history, goals, philosophies, and current needs. Encourage her to pursue a service project that interests her to help a charity.

A good role model puts God first, loves her family, serves others, has an attitude of compassion and forgiveness, is humble and modest, and speaks out against wrongdoing. Sit down with your family and talk about why these values are important and how to recognize them when they see them—on and off screen.

COFFEE BREAK

Think about how you can encourage your child to pursue his God-given gifts. Review Romans 12:6-8 together as you consider your child's strengths and brainstorm with him ways he can use his spiritual gifts today.

The average adult sees about three movies per month.

Talk to your kids about the fact that God gives each of us talents and that the actors we see in movies are no exception. Some are incredibly funny, while others are gifted at drama. Use this discussion as a springboard to ask your child how he thinks God has gifted him. If he's not sure, this is a terrific opportunity to share Romans 12:6-8 and help your child grow spiritually!

key point
REAL "STARS" PUT GOD FIRST!

When you're looking for role models, consider that many stars lend their names to projects or concerns they are interested in. Some also give of their time or money. Find out if your child's favorite actors are involved in a charity. If so, and if it's a cause you can support, help your child discover how he can help. Getting involved with a favorite star's charity is a great way to introduce your child to the many benefits of serving others!

When people were asked about movies, nearly half said that viewing movies is one of their two or three favorite types of entertainment.
(The Barna Group)

key point
USE GOD'S GIFTS WISELY.

Channel the TV in positive directions.

Although it seems shocking, the American Academy of Pediatrics recommends no more than one hour a day for children under four and *none at all* for kids under two. Even for older kids, too much time with the television has negative consequences.

TV is a terrible babysitter at any age.

Television can entertain and educate, but it can also be a convenient babysitter for parents of young children. One of the reasons well-intentioned parents turn on the tube is because we're busy and it's easy. But each hour your child spends in front of the television is an hour she isn't spending with her imagination and creativity, such as playing with modeling dough or a soccer ball.

MORE THAN HALF OF THE TV SHOWS AND SPORTS THAT ARE POPULAR WITH TEENAGERS HAVE ALCOHOL ADS OR SHOW ALCOHOL IN THE PROGRAMMING ITSELF!
(FTC REPORT, 1999)

According to the American Medical Association, underage drinking factors in nearly half of all teen car crashes and is linked to two-thirds of sexual assaults and date rapes of teens.

In addition, there are a myriad of reasons to be concerned about the messages your child is getting from his "friends" on TV. *CQ Researcher* reports that by the time most kids turn sixteen they'll have seen 75,000 ads for alcohol! Commercials can increase the likelihood of drinking according to the *American Journal of Public Health*. As parents, we can work to guard against the negative influences our kids are exposed to on TV and at the movies.

If that weren't enough to contemplate, the Center for Disease Control found that more than 60 percent of overweight children between the ages of five and ten already show at least one risk factor for heart disease. We're stacking the deck against our kids when we allow too much television!

Before you pull the plug and haul your television to the curb, remember that there are many shows whose characters are good role models for our kids. Explore nature shows to learn about exciting animals or check out cooking shows to find recipes your family may want to try. The key is to teach your kids to filter and to monitor what they watch and for you to model good TV-viewing habits!

PARENTS POINTER

Did you know that TV shows have ratings? Thanks to the V-Chip, parents can block certain shows based on their ratings. All TVs manufactured after January 2000 include the V-Chip (unless they're smaller than 13 inches). Consult your television's manual or on-screen menu to program yours!

key point

TV ISN'T A SAFE HAVEN.

key point

TV CREATES "LOST" TIME.

TIPS FOR TODDLERS
Provide your young child with a safe play area where she can learn to be creative with the toys and books she's given. This early training will make it easier to forgo using the TV as a baby-sitter when she is older.

CHANNEL THE TV IN POSITIVE DIRECTIONS.

41

Monitoring the monitor requires vigilance.

key point
PARENTS CONTROL THE REMOTE!

How we monitor our children's television viewing depends in part on the age of our children. For the youngest set, parents are in control choosing when and if we turn on the TV. As kids grow, they want to have more of a say. The key is guiding them to make good choices when they're young and watching together whenever possible.

One of the problems with kids and television is the amount of advertising that targets children. Companies pay to have their products placed in TV shows so your child can learn early on how "cool" it is to drink a certain brand of soda. One way to combat this intense marketing is to talk to your kids about the intent of advertising and product placement. When your child is aware that someone is trying to sell him something, he can become a more savvy consumer.

While children may master the art of the savvy consumer, it's still likely that they'll want to watch some shows that aren't on your personal top-ten list of favorites. Your child is trying to figure out how he fits into the big picture of the wider world. This is when communication and rules are vital. It's important for kids to understand the values driving our decisions. While they may still disagree with the rules, most will eventually respect them.

"Television has proved that people will look at anything rather than each other."

—Ann Landers

It's also imperative to set expectations. When your older child wants to watch a show that's not in line with your principles, hear her out or watch the show together. We don't want our children to turn off distasteful programs out of blind obedience. We want to raise them to make *good choices* when they're adults.

Terrific TV tips:

• **Take TVs out of bedrooms.**

• **Set time limits.**

• **Select specific programs to watch.**

• **Don't turn the TV on during dinner.**

• **Schedule family viewing time and enjoy programs together.**

TARGET MOMENT

Explain to your child that companies pay to display their products on popular shows. Creating this awareness is pivotal because most kids don't like to be "sold to." Then watch their favorite show and see who can identify the most product placements during the show or the most ads between segments.

key point
SET REALISTIC EXPECTATIONS.

Computers are a modern-day blessing and curse.

Computers and the Internet have made it easier to keep in touch, write papers, and renew library books. On the other hand, it has opened the door to potentially dangerous territory for our kids!

Surfing requires a tough advisory "board."

In pre-Internet days, our parents discouraged us from "loitering" when we weren't doing anything because it would lead to no good. Today we worry about which Internet sites and chat rooms our kids are visiting—the new method of loitering. National Public Radio (NPR) reported that 54 percent of children ages ten to seventeen visit chat rooms, and an astonishing 20 percent of our kids have been approached by a pedophile in a chat room!

BIG BIBLE POINT

"My son, if sinners entice you, do not give in to them" *(Proverbs 1:10).* **Print this verse and place it in a prominent place near your computer. Remind your child that God commands us to obey His guidelines and wants to keep us safe—even on the Net!**

Chat rooms are a popular place for kids, but they can also be dangerous. Kids need to know that people on the Web aren't necessarily who they say they are. Pedophiles can easily masquerade as peers or teenagers who share their likes and dislikes. Explore the sites your child is interested in and set ground rules regarding when and where they can access chat rooms.

89% of sexual solicitations were made in chat rooms or instant messages.
(PEW study reported in *JAMA*, 2001)

DON'T FORGET

Make sure your kids know these rules for safe Internet use:

• **Private is private. Don't give out your name, address, school name, or home or cell-phone numbers.**

• **Never plan a rendez-vous without telling Mom and Dad. If your kids make a legitimate friend online, arrange for all of you to meet in a restaurant or other public place.**

• **Don't open e-mail from unknown senders.**

• **Read** Child Safety on the Information Highway **(by Lawrence J. Magid at www.safekids.com/ child_safety.htm).**

key point
THE INTERNET ISN'T A SAFE PLAY-GROUND!

key point
DON'T LET KIDS ROAM FREELY ON THE NET.

An NPR survey found that almost one-third of kids ages have seen Internet pornography. Help your child understand that, just as in society, good and evil exist on the Web. Share these tips for handling uncomfortable situations online and allow your child to practice using each:

• *Immediately click the Back button on the browser.*
• *Tell you immediately so you can report the link that sent him to the offensive site.*
• *Discuss who your child can talk to in case he's reluctant to tell you about what he's seen.*

If your child tells you he's been approached online by a stranger or encounters pornographic material, reassure him he did the right thing in telling you. Then contact the National Center for Missing and Exploited Children at www.cybertipline.com or call 1-800-THE-LOST. While you can rest assured that most children will not encounter this type of danger, it's important to know what to do if it does happen!

COMFUTERS ARE A MODERN-DAY BLESSING AND CURSE.

Software can provide a hard shield to guard kids.

Despite the pitfalls of the Web, there's no need to despair. Check with your Internet Service Provider (ISP) for filtering software they offer. Companies like AOL and MSN offer some parental controls that are included in your monthly service fee.

You can also purchase content-blocking software programs online or at local software and office retailers. These programs restrict access to areas that are inappropriate for kids, such as certain types of Web sites and chat rooms. One well-reviewed and thorough program is CYBERsitter 9.0. When you're considering a Web-filtering program, you want: software that will block Web sites, chat rooms, newsgroups, e-mail, and instant messaging; the ability to customize the filters for each child; and a package you can easily update to keep up with changing technology and your growing child.

key point
SOFTWARE FILTERS HELP PROTECT KIDS!

COFFEE BREAK

Take a few minutes to become familiar with software to guard your kids! Check out:

CYBERsitter 9.0 (cybersitter. com or software4parents.com)

Norton Internet Security (amazon.com or software.com)

CyberPatrol (cyberpatrol.com)

DON'T FORGET

For more information and filtering reviews, check out

- www.getnetwise.org
- www.internetfilter-review.com
- www.cyberangels.org

Stop "e-loitering" and free surfing before they get started! Help your child find and bookmark safe sites in the following categories: a nature discovery site, a kids' site offering crafts and puzzles, a hobby site, and a homepage for a foreign country your child might enjoy learning about. Stick with these bookmarked pages only and switch them every couple of months to keep your child's interest.

While these programs offer great assistance to parents, no software program can filter everything. Some children are extremely savvy and can circumvent the filters we establish. Some of the people running objectionable sites want kids to find them and figure out how to slip past many filters.

key point
SOFTWARE FILTERS CAN'T REPLACE PARENTS!

Just as we watch over our youngsters at the playground, we must cast a watchful eye over their Internet use. Place the computer in a public area such as your den or kitchen. Never put a computer in your child's bedroom. If it's there now, take it out! Surf with younger kids when you can and monitor your older kids' Internet activity. This is one area predators are most likely to seek out kids—be in the room when they try to enter!

Video games aren't always child's play.

key point
VIDEO GAMES CAN BE EDUCATIONAL.

A popular pastime for kids is playing video games. Retailers know that from toddler programs with Barney and Arthur to adult programs with violent content, video games sell. Among the games that are purely entertainment, you'll find sports, action, fantasy, skill, and strategy-style games for kids of all ages.

If you're considering video games for your child, rest assured that the majority of games are not offensively violent. Kids can improve math and reading skills, master the basics of chess, and even practice basic investing! There are so many first-rate games for children that your primary role will be to find the ones that fit your child's needs and to monitor the time your child plays the games.

90% of U. S. homes
with kids
have rented or
owned a video or
computer game.
(J. Quittner, 1999)

If your child wants to play a video game that contains violence, ask him why the developers decided to give points for killing people and what tools they used to make it "fun." Then compare the action on screen to reality. Personalize the game by asking:

- *Would it be fun to hurt or kill someone?*

- *What if that person was someone's son, father, or neighbor?*

- *How many people would be affected by the death?*

key point
LIMIT TIME AND CONTENT OF GAMES.

What do those letters on the video game boxes mean?

EC (Early Childhood)—3 and older.

E (Everyone)—6 and older.

T (Teen)—13 and older.

Don't buy games with E or T ratings without checking into them first. Games rated M (mature), A (adult only), and RP (rating pending) are not for kids. For more details, read the ratings guide at www.esrb.org.

We've all heard about a possible connection between violent video games and violent children. Games that depict violence against women or toward fellow citizens or that encourage alcohol and tobacco abuse have no place in Christian homes—or with any children. Feeding minds with these destructive attitudes is potentially harmful, not only to kids' health but to their precious hearts!

Regardless of your child's age, work to establish time limits for video games and make sure there's still plenty of time to pursue other interests, like sports and reading. Work to establish content limits. Review ratings given by the Entertainment Software Rating Board (ESRB), which rates all video games. Apply your judgment, the most important rating of all, to each video game you consider.

Keep video games happy and healthy!

BIG BIBLE POINT

"The LORD detests the way of the wicked but he loves those who pursue righteousness" (Proverbs 15:9). **Explain to your child that not all video games are uplifting, honor God, or model the goodness God desires us to have in our lives. Remind your child that not all games are good for**

The Internet is a techno-tool to use wisely.

Given all of the threats video games and the Internet present, why bother with them? Because most kids use them and enjoy them, and it's unlikely that our kids will be the exception. Consider the positives: information, communication, education, and entertainment are at your child's instant disposal.

key point
COMPUTERS CAN CONNECT FAMILIES.

key point
THE INTERNET IS INFORMATIVE.

Make it a family activity to find fun activities on the Web. For parents of young children, Web sites abound with free coloring pages, dot-to-dots, and kid-friendly games. For 'tweens, focus on their interests. Does your child love books? If so, check out www.randomhouse.com. Does she want to know more about the Statue of Liberty? Go to www.google. com and type in "Statue of Liberty." 'Tweens can help plan the next family vacation by researching how to get there, what hotel options there are, and what to do once there.

TIPS FOR TODDLERS

Try these Web sites for fun, printable activities online.

• *www.akidsheart.com*
• *www.bigideafun.com*
• *www.first-school.ws*

Be sure to share the fun adventure with your toddler or preschooler—and provide lots of crayons and markers to complete the pages!

Have you caught the bug?

Many parents have gotten the "Internet bug" and spend hours online shopping, chatting, or surfing. Remember that too many hours spent online offers a poor role model for kids and sends the message that it's okay to isolate in front of the computer—sometimes at the expense of family time. Interact with your kids instead!

The usefulness of computers and the Internet aren't limited to family fun. A wealth of information is available for research projects or pursuing individual interests. A child interested in the space program can go to the NASA Web site and learn what it takes to be an astronaut or dream up a scientific experiment and enter a contest to have astronauts perform the experiment in space!

Educational and fun family activities aside, your kids can also use the Internet to connect with family members through e-mail and sending digital photos to keep in touch. Older kids can create family online scrapbooks of vacations, celebrations, and more to help scattered family members stay close. E-mail encourages kids to write notes and letters and feels less formal than paper writing.

TRY THIS!

Set aside some time this month to write to a grandparent, cousin, aunt, or uncle. Using e-mail makes communication quick. If your relatives don't have an account, break out the pen and paper! Kids can go the old-fashioned route for now.

Music can be the strongest media force!

Joshua 24:15 commands us to "choose for yourselves this day whom you will serve." It's a strong challenge to put God first, but no other challenge is as worthy! This short and simple verse reminds us that we must make an active choice to follow God. Part of following God is honoring him with our lives—and the music we listen to is no exception.

It's wise to be leery of lyrics.

key point
MUSIC INFLUENCES OUR FEELINGS.

The desire for a particular social status, vehicle to drive, or ideal weight on the scale can displace our desire for a close relationship with our Creator. What does music have to do with idolatry? More than you might think! Music is an influential part of our children's lives and has the power to slowly shape their perceptions. Proverbs 13:20 tells us that "he who walks with the wise grows wise." This is as true with our choice of music as it is for our friendships.

When kids choose music, be aware that CDs with explicit lyrics are marketed to children as young as twelve, according to a report by the Federal Trade Commission. The music industry *voluntarily* puts stickers on CDs with offensive lyrics, but most stores still allow kids to purchase CDs with an "Explicit Content" sticker. The use of violence, glamorization of alcohol and drug use, and permissive attitudes toward sex are prevalent in song lyrics— and disconcerting.

Watch a music video with your kids. Afterwards, talk about how it made each of you feel. Discuss how what you saw conflicts or agrees with what God teaches us about honoring Him and serving others.

Music with negative lyrics can prey upon the already-disturbed child. It's not news that impressionable youth look for companions who will understand them, and they may think they've found them when they hear the violent, suicidal messages of some musical artists. The National School Safety Center has a checklist for violent youth at www.nssc1.org. If you have any reason to worry, download this checklist now!

key point
CHECK OUT LYRICS CAREFULLY!

> Teen buyers of Christian music were as likely as other teens to engage in music piracy. This included teens who purchased contemporary Christian music (77% had committed an act of piracy), gospel recordings (80%), and worship music (80%).
>
> (The Barna Group, 2004)

The bottom line is that we need to be involved. We can listen to lyrics, watch videos, and take our kids to the symphony—but we can't force them to like a particular style of music. We *can* teach them to discern negative messages and to guard their minds so that even when they're grown up, they will look for positive music and media.

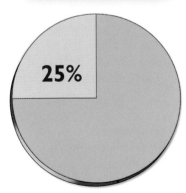

Nearly 75 percent of 12- to 19-year-olds are watching these same videos!

Nearly 25 percent of the music videos on a popular music TV station show alcohol and drug use!

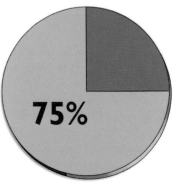

Make music a feel-good experience.

When our kids listen to positive music, they experience joy and peace and perhaps even do better in school! That's right—a highly publicized study at the University of California, Irvine, found that children who took a test after listening to Mozart for ten minutes showed an increase in their spatial reasoning skills. This isn't news to many preschool and elementary teachers, who have used songs to help kids learn for years.

TIPS FOR 'TWEENS

Positive music makes you feel ...
- Joy
- Hope
- Good about yourself
- Good about others

Negative music makes you feel ...
- Pain or anger
- Misunderstood
- Not cool enough
- Too cool or better than others

Make a list of your own favorite songs and musicians. Evaluate your choices in light of what you're teaching your children. If you choose to make some changes, use the Internet to look up this year's best-selling Christian artists. For example, check out www. christianmusic.about.com.

Comforting melodies can also help ease stress. Whether we pop in a favorite CD on the way home from work or while we relax in a hot bath, positive music has the power to relax us. Helping kids learn to use music in constructive ways when they're young doesn't guarantee they won't experiment with negative music later, but it provides them with a safe base to which they can return.

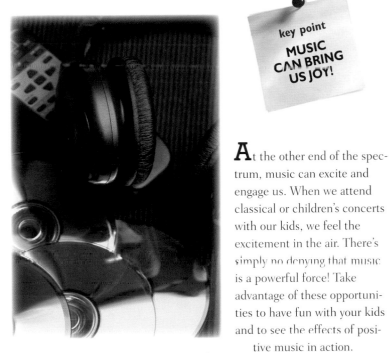

key point
MUSIC CAN BRING US JOY!

At the other end of the spectrum, music can excite and engage us. When we attend classical or children's concerts with our kids, we feel the excitement in the air. There's simply no denying that music is a powerful force! Take advantage of these opportunities to have fun with your kids and to see the effects of positive music in action.

key point
POSITIVE MUSIC RELAXES US.

As you share different types of music with your child, discuss the range of emotions that songs make us feel. Talking with your child about the pros and cons of different musical styles can help her celebrate music that honors God, makes her feel joyous, and sends lively, positive messages!

Media and Its Impact

Once our are kids old enough to leave home for play dates or school, we can be sure our messages and teaching aren't the only ones they hear. From the time they're very young, our kids are barraged with suggestions, some that advocate and others that conflict with God's perfect plan.

Media impacts cultures.

Books, magazines, movies, and music commiserate with our kids about teenage troubles, give them "advice" on relationships, and sometimes glorify the use of drugs, alcohol, and violence. These media messages play a part in shaping who our children become.

Sex and body image often come from media.

One of the things you probably worry about is whether or not your child perceives himself in a positive light. But how many of us have expressed dissatisfaction with our own bodies? We're as influenced by the media as our kids, and our examples are vital as we struggle to negate the unrealistic standards set by many models and actors.

"I'd be happier if I was only thinner..."

Two-thirds of preteen and teenage girls believe their lives would be better if they were thinner.

Researchers at Columbia University's Graduate School of Journalism found that models today weigh an average of 23 percent less than the rest of us! Even girls who don't resort to starvation may feel discontented and devalued when measured against this slender yardstick.

Our children are bombarded with sexual messages and imagery. The American Academy of Pediatrics warns that the average child will be exposed to nearly 14,000 references to sex in the media each year, with few mentioning the dangers of contracting a sexually transmitted disease or unwanted pregnancies.

According to one recent study, the more time preteens and teens spend watching soap operas, movies, and music videos, the higher their degree of body dissatisfaction. The message our kids hear is that media's contrived idea of an "ideal" body type is the right one—but that's deadly wrong! Remind your child that people are literally dying to be thin. Tell your child not to let media bully him or her into starvation; media doesn't care about us, but God does!

BIG BIBLE POINT

"So God created man in his own image, in the image of God he created him" (Genesis 1:27). **Remind your child that God made us, that God doesn't make junk, and that we can take joy in His creation! We should care for the bodies God gave us, but it's not necessary to pursue a Hollywood or Madison Avenue ideal.**

key point
MEDIA CAN CREATE FALSE REALITIES!

Pray for your child as he starts his day and as you tuck him in at night. Be involved in your child's life: know his friends, his hobbies, and how he spends his free time. Work to remind your child that God judges a person by the goodness in one's heart, not by outward appearances (1 Samuel 16:7). Remind your child that our value lies in Christ and in serving others with God's love—not in one's body size!

Stereotypes are affected by the media.

If we think back far enough, most of us can remember the "popular" girls and boys in our high schools. Recall for a moment what you can about one of the popular kids at your school. Was he attractive and funny? Was she kind or mean-spirited? Now ask yourself if you truly knew that person—or just the image?

One problem with stereotypes in music, movies, and television is that they present our kids with a one-dimensional picture. If your child describes someone using a stereotype, suggest that she get to know this person a little better. You don't want to force a friendship but to persuade her that there is more to a person than a stereotype suggests.

key point
LABELING CREATES CONFUSION.

TIPS FOR TODDLERS

Help your young child develop her analytical skills from the get-go. When the "scary monster" in her favorite book is red, talk about whether all red monsters are scary. Ask her if this particular red monster is always scary and why she likes him.

key point
STEREOTYPES ARE HARMFUL.

BIG BIBLE POINT

"You intended to harm me, but God intended it for good to accomplish what is now being done, the saving of many lives" (Genesis 50:20). **If your child has suffered from stereotyping, remind her that God can use hurtful situations to bring about good.**

Stereotypes create expectations of behavior—and they're usually wrong! A more harmful outcome occurs when movie or television characters perpetuate prejudicial stereotypes. Negative depictions of minorities as thugs and drug dealers are as damaging for those being stereotyped as they are for viewers who believe them!

> Get your child to think critically by giving these examples of stereotypes. Have your child tell why he thinks they're not true and how they could create confusing ideas. Remind your child that stereotypes created by what we see or read are untrue and can hurt others.
> - *Blondes aren't smart.*
> - *Redheads have bad tempers.*
> - *Kids are noisy.*
> - *Big dogs are mean.*

We can turn the tables on stereotypes by using them to talk to our kids about the work God does in each of our lives. For example, when kids see a stern female lawyer on television who appears cold, it suggests that successful, driven women lack warmth. Instead of accepting this as a given reality, think about where her motivation may come from. Did God create her with a special energy? Think about how this lawyer might show her nurturing side outside of the office. Examining these questions helps children question stereotypes when they see them.

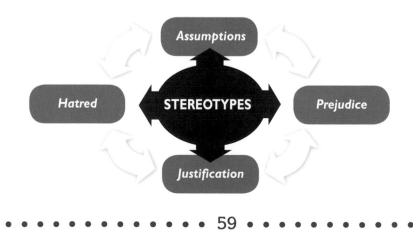

Assumptions

Hatred   STEREOTYPES   Prejudice

Justification

Media impacts our opinions.

While there are a great many differences of opinion in our society, certain situations evoke almost universal reactions. Following September 11, 2001, our hearts ached for our country. These reactions were based partially on our collective values, which are in some measure shaped by the movies and newspapers we share.

Media can desensitize us.

Have you ever heard a loud noise over and over again so that after a while you actually blocked it out? This is called "desensitization." The more we see robberies, violence, war, and criminal acts in the media, the more we tend to become desensitized to them; the less shocking they are. The desensitization process begins very early in life these days!

key point
JESUS PROMOTED PEACE.

key point
ON-SCREEN VIOLENCE ISN'T CHILD'S PLAY.

> **Consider these verses and how they relate to exposing kids to violence:**
> "Blessed are the peacemakers, for they will be called sons of God" (Matthew 5:9) and "Even a child is known by his actions, by whether his conduct is pure and right" (Proverbs 20:11).

A study at the University of Michigan showed that boys who watched vast amounts of TV violence were significantly more likely to grow up to be men who used force to get their way. This fact alone should give us pause—as well as an incentive to curtail our kids' access to these types of music videos, games, and shows.

DON'T FORGET

- Limit your child's exposure to media.
- Screen what your child watches.
- Watch or play together when you can.
- Keep the TV out of your child's bedroom.
- Place computers and TVs in high-traffic areas.

According to one study, 20 percent of the most popular video games today contain violence against women. Playing games and committing violence aren't the same, but these games do send a message!

Violence on TV or in movies is usually presented in a way that trivializes the outcome or glamorizes the perpetrator. Our kids need to understand that real violence is complex and involves suffering and sadness by the victim. The more frequently our kids see weapons and violence, the more "normal" it seems.

In stark contrast, Jesus brought a message of peace. He didn't teach us to seek vengeance but to pray for those who persecute us. He didn't tell us to strike back but to turn the other cheek. When Jesus came to bridge the divide between our sinful natures and God's kingdom, He brought a spirit of compassion worth emulating. When our kids manage their time and evaluate their choices in light of Jesus' teachings, media can have a less dangerous place in their lives.

PARENTS POINTER

Don't dismiss video-game warnings because your kids are "just playing sports games." A 1998 study by Simon Fraser University showed that kids develop a propensity for gaming, which can become stumbling blocks when they're older.

Media can sway our system of values.

There's a code of conduct for each of our families that sets the tone and mood of our homes and creates an atmosphere that's uniquely ours. Whether we're CNN diehards or prefer to skim the latest issue of *Focus on the Family* magazine, media's pervasiveness influences these values. As it does, it can make incremental changes in society's views as a whole and ultimately affect the values our kids adopt.

key point
MEDIA CAN
CONTRADICT
OUR VALUES.

One of the things families might enjoy watching together on TV are sporting events. Regrettably, this is also one area where our children receive negative messages and see distorted values. When kids discover that a top-notch athlete has used steroids, the message they hear is that they can achieve greatness, too, with a little help from this illegal and potentially dangerous substance.

DON'T FORGET

Movies and TV shows aren't the only places our kids encounter images and language that contradict many Christian values. We should evaluate all media, including:

• Internet

• magazines

• video games

• music videos

• music lyrics

COFFEE BREAK

• Do you model positive values by your actions or only by your words?

• How do your values match those God desires us to have?

• Do your media choices match your values?

• How can you make wiser media choices this week?

Misbehaving movie stars and musical artists give our kids another skewed view of the world and their own values. It's important for kids to realize that when media contradicts their personal values, they must ignore the messages and stand strong with their values intact!

Many preteens struggle to exert their own autonomy. They may resent being "told" what values they're to have and may even test the waters by rebelling and modeling different behaviors. Listen to your kids' opinions about media and guide them in coming to their own conclusions about the values they see and hear and what they know in their hearts is right. Forcing your opinion with disregard to theirs only creates distance—and dissent!

While we can't hide children away from messages that are contradictory to our values, we can educate them and try to reduce the negative influences on them. We should encourage our kids to compare and contrast the messages they see and hear to our values and to the particular circumstances. Help your child be aware that media's messages don't always coincide with our personal values and that we must guard against imitating what we see and hear and instead stand firm in the values God desires us to have!

key point
MEDIA CAN CREATE ALTERED REALITY.

Kids often express themselves through what they see and hear!

Media impacts our choices.

We make hundreds of small choices every week when we purchase toothpaste and laundry detergent or when we rent movies. Older kids make choices about the clothes they wear and the music they buy. Part of media literacy is knowing what we're being sold and when.

Add discretion to marketing ads.

Whiter teeth can make you happier? Don't believe all the ads you see or hear!

This is a good time to examine your own buying habits. Do you buy from a list or tend to impulse shop? Take a hard look at your purchasing behaviors and how media influences them.

Kids are big business! A report by MarketResearch.com indicates that five- to fourteen-year-olds spend $40 billion of their own money each year and influence $146 billion more! Some commercials tell kids how cool they'll be when wearing their clothes, and soft-drink companies assure kids that the hip prefer *their* cola. And teeth whitening ads convince us we'll be more attractive with their product!

So how do we teach our kids that they don't necessarily need what is being sold? Explain that companies make money when we buy what they sell—and they want to sell us as much as they can. Discuss *why* companies want us to buy their products. Helping kids understand the profit motive also lays the groundwork for smarter budgeting when they manage their own finances!

BIG BIBLE POINT

Read aloud Philippians 4:19 with your child, then discuss the following questions:

• Who can supply what we need and want?
• Why do companies want us to buy everything from them?
• Why is wanting or buying everything we see not being good stewards with money?
• Do you believe every commercial you see? Explain.

Remind your child that companies pay to advertise and that much of what we see and hear has been "bought" and aimed at us. Point out that God provides for us because He loves us—not because we're consumers He wants to please!

TARGET MOMENT

Have family members take turns acting out their favorite TV commercials. Let everyone guess what the commercial is and what's being sold. Then decide if the commercial is realistic, fantasy, or just plain silly. Remind children that watching television commercials tests our critical thinking and how gullible certain companies think we are!

Once our kids have mastered analyzing commercials, they can begin to apply their skills to other media. Ask your child to watch for brand logos on sports items hanging at the hockey arena. What about ads on the Internet? Just noticing these types of advertising can create awareness in our kids and help them become smarter consumers.

Another subtle form of advertising is product placement or logos companies have paid to place in favorite movies and television shows. Remind your child that many advertising claims simply aren't true, but companies want you to believe them anyway. Critical thinking helps our kids recognize the often false or exaggerated messages behind the marketing!

key point
ADS REQUIRE CRITICAL THINKING!

Media creates "good" versus "bad" choices.

Our kids' lives are filled with moments when they must decide which path to choose. For kids, a lesson looms. For us, the choice is whether to let our children live with the impending consequences. As difficult as it may be, we give our children a priceless gift when we allow them to accept the consequences of their choices. It helps them learn fundamental lessons and encourages them to make wise decisions as they grow.

key point
GUIDE KIDS'
MEDIA
CHOICES.

Your child will have to make many decisions regarding what she listens to, reads, and watches in the years to come. To ensure that our kids are ready to make wise media choices, we need to get them involved in the decision-making process. Our objectives should be to help our kids understand and, eventually, embrace the values that determine why we permit the shows and games that we do.

Keep your kids busy and they'll spend less time in front of the computer, the television, and video games. Here are some active things you can do with kids of all ages:

- *Take a nature walk.*
- *Visit the zoo or library.*
- *Bake cookies for a teacher or neighbor.*
- *Play board games or word games.*
- *Read a short story together.*
- *Organize a toy chest or cupboard.*
- *Write newsy notes to relatives.*
- *Plant a garden or paint flowerpots.*

PARENTS POINTER

When kids make poor decisions, avoid an "I told you so" mentality and put the decision squarely on their shoulders. Encouraging kids to problem solve helps them to develop an attitude of ownership and responsibility—even in their media choices!

Getting kids involved in the decision-making process also gives them a chance to learn more about themselves and the consequences of their choices. Naturally, we should point out pros and cons for choices, but if we permit our kids to choose in spite of our warnings, they learn valuable lessons about the consequences of their decisions.

We want to responsibly screen media choices ahead of time so we can make age-appropriate selections that meet our family's unique criteria. Children don't have the maturity to understand the multifaceted themes of grown-up shows, which can skew kids' perception of reality. It's important to guide children's choices in media and to help them recognize that all decisions have consequences, both good and bad.

key point

CHOICES LEAD TO CONSE-QUENCES.

✓

Screen it! See what others have to say about the content of movies before your kids see them. Check out www.screenit.com and www.pluggedin-online.com.

Media impacts our personal habits and time.

How often have you heard your son utter phrases he's heard in a movie or your daughter flaunt an attitude she saw on TV? They like to imitate their heroes, their friends, and their friends' heroes—too much at times!

Language and behaviors are often media-modeled.

key point
MEDIA ISN'T ALWAYS GOOD TO IMITATE!

key point
KIDS IMITATE WHAT THEY SEE AND HEAR.

Of the many ways we see media's influence on kids, their language is one of the most evident. An amusing example was given recently in a study Scott F. Kiesling published at the University of Pittsburgh. Most of us have heard the word "dude" and may have used it ourselves, but it hasn't always been hip. After its frequent use in the hit 1982 movie *Fast Times at Ridgemont High* (Universal Pictures) the word "dude" entered the wider vernacular. While this example is entertaining, there are many other phrases and uses of words that are less humorous.

In movies and TV shows, for example, we frequently hear the Lord's name taken in vain and other expletives shouted for effect. Even without regard to religious ethics and morals, we should teach our children that using such words reveals a lack of wisdom. Kids with a strong command of vocabulary don't need expletives.

BIG BIBLE POINT

Sometimes older kids, having been influenced by our culture, dismiss the importance of not taking the Lord's name in vain or "swearing" on something. Read aloud Matthew 5:34-37 and discuss why a simple "yes" or "no" is better than swearing an oath.

Other concerns about media exposure include its effect on alcohol and tobacco use. The American Academy of Pediatrics advises us that 52 percent of eighth-graders admit they have tried alcohol. The Centers for Disease Control says that each day 4,000 American kids start smoking. Think of all the beer ads during "wholesome" sports shows. Our kids are repeatedly exposed to the idea that drinking and smoking are cool whether they see it in print or on the big screen.

TIPS FOR 'TWEENS
Give your child an "old-fashioned thesaurus (in book form). Kids can rely on a computer thesaurus when writing school papers, but it won't be available when they're talking with friends. To be able to use words effectively, they'll need to have them in their vocabularies!

11 Billion

2 Billion

Dollars spent per year on media advertising.

Watching TV can be harmful to your health.

Media influences that model negative habits of behavior, slang, or foul language do affect our kids—for the worse. Choose media carefully. Remind your child that God desires what's best for us and that He desires us to make Him our first focus and best habit!

Health can be affected by media choices.

TIPS FOR 'TWEENS

Challenge your child to "earn" minutes of TV viewing time by exchanging exercising for TV minutes. For example, a half-hour of TV viewing might equal 20 sit-ups or a 20-minute walk around the block before the show starts. Kids will learn to make choices and to plan ahead—and may find themselves shaping up as they view their favorite shows!

In addition to the dangers of smoking and drinking, media can affect our health. Excessive television viewing has been linked to obesity in children, but it's not just the inactivity that leads to excess. Think about the foods, drinks, and snacks that are advertised. Does your child see a lot of commercials for carrots and apples? Unless he's watching some very different programming than most kids, ads for fast food, colas, and sugary cereals are more common fare.

According to the National Eating Disorder Association, as many as 81 percent of ten-year-olds fear being overweight. How many times a day do our kids face the juxtaposition of unhealthy advertised food with unrealistically thin actresses on the shows these ads support? The figures of many "fashionable" actresses are beyond reach for most healthy eaters, much less kids feasting on sugar for breakfast, fries for lunch, and munchies in front of the TV!

Drugs and substance abuse are other entice-ments found in media. The rap artist Eminem has received a lot of attention for his graphic lyrics, but you may be shocked to find out exactly what *graphic* means. In "Role Model" he instructs kids to "follow me and … smoke weed, take pills, drop outta school, kill people, and drink." A whole host of artists extol drug use and sexual escapades. Again, our media choices have good and bad consequences for our physical, as well as our mental, health!

In 2003, Americans consumed an aver-age of fifty 12-oz cans of soda per month, according to the American Beverage Asso-ciation, and much of that pop was shared with TV and movie time!

Using media *can* be part of a healthy lifestyle, too! Try going for a walk or exercising with your child as you listen to lively music. Provide healthy snacks to enjoy as you watch TV. Purchase a family stationary bike and take turns pedaling as you watch cartoons. Teach your child good judgment by establishing guidelines and setting positive exam-ples of using media in healthy ways.

in a typical year kids spend …
- **1,500 hours watching TV**
- **33 hours conversing with parents**

That's 4 hours a day with TV and only 5 minutes inter-acting with parents!

In *Fast Food Nation* (**Houghton Mifflin, 2001**), **author Eric Schlosser finds that Americans spent $110 billion on fast food in 2001! Next month, help your kids track how much comes from their wallets. If they're willing to forgo fast food the fol-lowing month, they can choose a charity to donate the money to instead!**

Media impacts our sense of reality.

The people who create movies, magazines, books, and TV shows create a fantasy world that often feels real, particularly to children who can't always recognize the fine line between fact and fiction. As we help our kids discern what's real and what's "reality" on the screen, they'll learn about how values affect decisions.

Reality TV isn't real.

Reality TV is everywhere, and it's clear to grown-ups that these shows aren't very real at all. Kids define the world and reality by the parameters of their limited experiences. They simply don't have the resources or maturity required to take these shows with a grain of salt.

BIG BIBLE POINT

Kids need to understand that the relentless pursuit of money leads to trouble. Discuss these verses and have your child tell why reality shows with prize money don't fit into God's plans of good stewardship.

- 1 Timothy 6:10
- Matthew 6:21
- Matthew 6:24

One myth perpetuated on these shows is that attractive people are automatically compatible. Participants make quick assumptions about each other and discover "love" within the allotted number of episodes. This distorts reality—and the precious nature of love as God intended. Despite what's depicted on TV, love isn't about two "perfect" people lounging in a hot tub!

key point

REALITY SHOWS AREN'T REALITY!

COFFEE BREAK

If you're "hooked" on a reality show ...

- Is this a reality you'd like in your own life? Why or why not?
- What good things does the show teach or model?
- What negative things does the show teach or model?
- What messages do you send to your child by watching each week?

key point

THE "REAL" PRIZE IS ETERNAL LIFE.

Another common element of reality TV is that money is the ultimate prize. When our kids seek to obey God and understand His purpose for them, it doesn't guarantee them an easy road full of prize money, but it promises the ultimate reality prize: spending eternity with Him!

Reality TV is filled with images that project a false picture of reality, but it doesn't stand alone. For years, dramas, sitcoms, and soap operas have been characterized by similar falsehoods and illusions of reality. We want our kids to realize that what they see in this type of programming isn't reality at all, that reality is God in our lives and our lives spent honoring Him!

Your real life as a family is much more interesting and rewarding than any reality show!

Draw lines between media fact and fantasy.

Some books are clearly fantasy, like *Lord of the Rings* by J. R. R. Tolkien (Houghton Mifflin). Others, like *John Adams* by David McCullough (Simon & Schuster), describe fact. Helping kids learn to discern fact from fantasy is important, and the first step is reminding them to verify the "facts."

When our children are old enough to watch the TV news or read newspapers and magazines, we need to teach them to develop a healthy skepticism without creating kids who have a deep-seated mistrust of authority figures. Instead, the goal is for our kids to respect authority, appreciate good ethics, recognize integrity—and discern fact from fiction.

TRY THIS!

Have the whole family review the important differences between fact and fantasy by doing a little artwork. Challenge everyone to draw one fantasy picture and one picture that shows something real. After the pictures are done, hold them up one by one and have everyone guess if it's a picture of fact or fantasy and why. Remind everyone why knowing the difference between fact and fiction is so important when it comes to choosing—and believing—media.

Make-believe is fun! But help your child separate fact from fantasy in media.

key point
CHECK FOR FACTS.

key point
REALIZE THAT "FACT" MAY BE FANTASY!

The next time you read a bedtime story to your child, ask him if the story is real and why or why not. Encourage your child to identify the facts or the fantasies in the story. Remind your child that not everything we see, hear, or read is true. Point out to your child that make-believe stories are fun even if we know they aren't true, but it's always important to know the difference between real and make-believe!

To give a good example of how truth can be distorted in the media, try dissecting local or national election ads with your older child. Prior to scrutinizing campaign ads, have your child research one of the candidate's views. Then contrast the actual views to the views an opponent attributes to him or her during the campaign.

TIPS FOR TODDLERS

Help your toddler or preschooler make a book so he can understand that people create stories and characters. Act out the story after it's written!

Your child is not too young to start learning about or remembering the differences between fact and fantasy. Teach your preschooler that what she sees on *Veggie Tales* isn't real, though it still is fun. Film your own make-believe movie or factual report on an animal. When kids create and film their own shows, fact or fiction, it helps them recognize the lines between fact and fantasy.

Mediating Choices

All children eventually make their own choices, including decisions about the role media plays in their lives. Naturally, we all hope our kids will make wise choices! To get them started in the right direction, we can pray for them, teach them to weigh their options and use resources to guide their decisions, and—as always—make sure they see us practicing what we preach!

Keep an eye on the time.

Making conscious decisions about the content of the media we use and the amount of time we devote to it teaches our kids that they have the power to control media's place in their lives.

Choose when to enjoy media.

key point
SCHEDULING MEDIA IS WISE.

TRY THIS!

During their newly found free time, encourage kids to work on interests and hobbies or play active games like hide-and-seek or soccer.

Before we expect our kids to curb the amount of time they spend watching TV or playing video games, we need to examine our own habits. Even with such hectic lives, we squander time by watching an additional TV show or shopping online for an extra hour before bedtime. If this sounds familiar, it's time to make a date with your television.

A date? Absolutely! We can schedule media time just like any other event. Once you've straightened out your own media habits, it's time to tackle the kids' routines. How much time do your kids spend playing computer games, watching TV, or surfing the Internet each week? Work together to develop a viewing plan everyone can live with while respecting the values that define your family.

Assess your children's daily activities and calculate the hours they have left to complete homework, help with chores, and simply play or relax. Out of those remaining hours, help them decide how much time to allot for media use and which modes of media they most enjoy. Remind your child that with each choice comes consequences. If he chooses to view a TV show, it may mean less time on the computer!

TIPS FOR TODDLERS

Avoid commercials by taping television shows before letting your child watch them or by opting to show age-appropriate videos. Be sure you schedule time to share a book or learn a new song.

TIPS FOR 'TWEENS

If your 'tween has an earphone growing out of her head, help her keep music in perspective by asking her these questions as guidelines for listening to music:

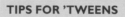

• *Can I glorify Christ by listening to this song or music?*

• *Am I using my time wisely by listening to this music?*

• *What has control over me and over my time?*

Whether to use or not to use media is an important choice. Tonight, turn off the electronic "toys" and choose to spend time with your child instead!

Choose how long to enjoy media.

Aren't you sometimes amazed at how long your kids can spend with television, video games, or the Internet? Children have an amazing propensity to just sit and be entertained. When we allow our kids to use these kinds of media, not only do we need to be aware of the content, but we must also define acceptable time limits for these pursuits.

WARNING!

- **Poor school performance**
- **Hitting or pushing other kids often**
- **Aggressively talking back to adults**
- **Frequent nightmares**
- **Increased eating of unhealthy foods**
- **Smoking, drinking, or drug use**

Watch for these side effects. They may mean that your child is making excessive or inappropriate media choices. If you're concerned, discuss it with your child or your child's doctor.

As you and your family discuss how long to spend with your favorite games and shows in the coming weeks, keep in mind that it's fair to use a sliding scale. If you haven't set strict limits before, start by cutting down on one or two shows a week. Invite each family member to name one show he would like to see and encourage everyone to share in the choices.

key point
TODDLERS DON'T NEED TV!

Make sure you do a reality check with your new rules. You don't want a severe new system that suffocates your child or nudges her toward rebellion!

TIPS FOR TODDLERS

Make the time your kids spend with media productive by investing in computer software that makes learning fun. Letters, numbers, and shapes are fun for toddlers and preschoolers.

The American Academy of Pediatrics recommends elementary-aged children spend no more than two hours a day in front of a screen (this means any kind of screen—TV, computer, or video game), and if they're under two years old, none at all. There's no need to be legalistic, though. Exceptions can and should be made for special events. And of course, computers may be required for educational studies. As long as you return to your plan afterwards, occasionally spending a few extra hours with media won't permanently change your family's habits.

PARENTS POINTER

Develop a viewing and listening contract to limit the times and types of media you use. For example, elementary-aged kids may limit media usage to two hours a day—and that is a total for all media use! Kids must then choose accordingly, such as a half hour for the computer, a half hour for TV, and an hour for music. Have everyone sign and date the media contracts. Infringements may mean only half time for the next two days! Use the following suggested time limits:

3-5 years	1 hour per day
6-9 years	1 1/2 hours per day
10-12 years	2 hours per day
13-18 years	2 1/2 hours per day
adults	3 hours per day

Media ratings make for clearer choices.

A trip to any media superstore can be daunting. The sheer volume of CDs and video games available can overwhelm all but the most techno-savvy parents. Kids tend to love these places, so we need to understand what we're looking for when we visit. Ratings are a good place to start.

Ratings are in place for a reason.

key point
DO YOUR RATINGS RESEARCH!

Movie ratings have been around since the Motion Picture Academy of America began its rating system in 1968. PG-13 was added in 1984. PG movies may contain strong language and sexual innuendoes. PG-13 movies are permitted to contain nudity, profanity, violence, and sexually derived words. Carefully check out your choice of movies to avoid any startling surprises!

Movie RATINGS

(According to the Motion Picture Academy of America.)

G—*General Audiences (no inappropriate material)*

PG—*Parental Guidance Suggested (prescreen for young children)*

PG-13—*Parental Guidance Cautioned (prescreen for preteens)*

R—*Restricted (under 17 only with adult)*

NC-17—*Restricted (under 17 not allowed)*

CD RATINGS

(Not required to state on CDs)

Parental Advisory Label *(contains explicit content)*

Edited Version Label *(explicit material has been modified or omitted)*

Video Game RATINGS

(According to the Entertainment Software Rating Board)

EC—*Early Childhood (no inappropriate material)*

E—*Everyone (may contain minimal violence, some comic mischief)*

T—*Teen (may contain violent content, strong language)*

M—*Mature (may contain adult themes, strong language, sexual content)*

AO—*Adults Only (may include graphic depictions of sex and/or violence; not intended for persons under 18)*

RP—*Rating Pending (awaiting final rating)*

If you're not familiar with TV ratings, you can find descriptions online at www.tvguidelines.org/ratings.asp. Use the ratings in conjunction with a V Chip to block material you find inappropriate. (The V stands for violence.) On screen, the ratings appear in the upper left-hand corner at the start of each program.

CDs and video games are rated, too, although compliance is not required or regulated. CDs that contain explicit content carry the Parental Advisory Label. The other label you may see is an Edited Version Label, which indicates that the album's explicit material has been modified. As for video games, the Entertainment Software Rating Board (ESRB) gives a two-part rating to each video game it reviews: the age-based rating and a description of the contents.

Ratings for movies, CD lyrics, TV shows, and video games serve as a guide to the content contained therein. It's important to understand the ratings as a baseline to begin your assessment. Don't rely entirely on ratings to make your decisions about what's permissible. There are a number of Web sites that help parents evaluate movies, music, and video games so you can decide which ones are appropriate for your family. The key to choosing any of these forms of media is to know your kids, define your family's values, and do your research!

R̶x What's another prescription for safe viewing? Getting a second ratings opinion from the American Academy of Pediatrics! Log on to www.aap.org/family/ratingsgame.htm and read their detailed ratings statement and descriptions.

DON'T FORGET

You have the power, and the responsibility, to stay informed about the content of the media your child is choosing. You wouldn't buy a book for yourself without first reading the back blurb. Don't purchase or rent media for your child without first checking out the label and the ratings!

TARGET MOMENT

Visit www.dove.org/reviews for movie reviews by the nonprofit Dove Foundation that promotes "wholesome family entertainment."

Share responsibility for media decisions.

Ideally, if we teach our children to analyze TV, movies, and musical lyrics from the time they're young, these lessons will pay big dividends when they're older. As you are no doubt aware, it doesn't always work this way. We're real parents with real kids, and all of us make mistakes. Kids will choose media we disagree with. How we react can affect our relationship with them as well as their future decisions.

> "Don't you wish there were a knob on the TV to turn up the intelligence? There's one marked 'Brightness...' but it doesn't work."
> —Gallagher

So what do you do when your child makes a poor media choice? This is one of those scenarios where there isn't a one-size-fits-all answer! Let's say you disagree with an R-rated movie your sixth-grader chooses. What can you do to guide his choices?

TARGET MOMENT

Take time to share in your child's favorite music, video games, movies, and TV shows. Here are a few tips that will help you share in your child— and his media choices!

- Listen to and discuss your child's opinions about media.
- Respect your child's individualism.
- Evaluate all media your child brings home.
- Share viewing and listening time!

DON'T FORGET

You are the
primary influence in
your child's life—
not his
media choices!

COFFEE BREAK

Can you name the last
three movies your child
watched? Do you know
how she felt about
them? Find out and
make a date to watch
the next one together!

key point
**POOR
CHOICES CAN
CREATE RICH
LEARNING.**

key point
**GUIDE—NOT
BULLY—
DECISIONS.**

First, allow your child to articulate the reasons why he wants to see the film, then carefully listen to his response. Next, honestly evaluate your stance. Once you've given it some thought, you have three choices: disallow the film, overlook the fact that your child watches it, or agree to disagree.

There will be certain instances when the first response is entirely appropriate. As parents, we have veto power and should use it judiciously. The second choice (looking the other way) is neither a good nor a desirable option. Choosing the latter (agreeing to disagree) can be viable. When you agree to disagree it means that you discuss the issues you have with the movie, then allow your child to see it with you. Having in-depth discussions rather than disagreements provides significant insight into your child. Share the decisions; share the communication!

Make media an interactive family event.

Media presents us with many wonderful opportunities to spend time with and discover more about the inner lives of our children. Using and discussing media as a family gives us access to these priceless insights.

Choose to look and listen with your kids.

key point
MEDIA CAN
ENCOURAGE
SHARING.

There is an inherent danger of isolation that comes with media use. Books, the Internet, and headphones are obviously isolating. However, even when we watch movies or listen to music with our kids, they are still alone with their thoughts. It may seem insensitive, but our job is to pry in a way that doesn't seem like prying.

Thought-provoking stories with well-developed characters communicate something about the value of integrity to our kids. Stories of redemption teach kids about failure and forgiveness. When we talk about the ideas portrayed in a show or story, it gives us a chance to add our own perceptions and thoughts. Hearing what other family members think can mitigate the influences of these messages because it invites our kids to recognize and consider other points of view.

Make it a family event—share what you see and think!

Almost every form of media communicates some sort of life message, and it isn't always positive or overt. We need to listen to our kids carefully to ascertain what they're hearing. Part of guiding them through the process of media means doing our homework and making good choices!

COFFEE BREAK

The old adage proves true: actions speak louder than words. When we spend time with our kids, we tell and assure them of their importance in our lives!

BIG BIBLE POINT

Watching movies and TV shows as a family offers great opportunities for evaluating behaviors that are positive or negative in God's eyes. After viewing shows with moral dilemmas, read aloud Matthew 5:3-11 (the Beatitudes) and together evaluate the characters' actions and decisions

key point
LOOK AND LISTEN WITH YOUR KIDS!

Doing our homework means we can't rely entirely on anyone or anything else (like ratings) to protect our children. We can, however, locate credible sources that review movies, music, TV shows, and video games. We can help kids apply family values to each movie and CD under consideration. Making good choices means the content of our own media choices should exemplify the standards to which we hold our kids' media choices.

Create your own media events.

Think about media from the creation side. Typically we watch a movie, but directors, producers, and actors are actively involved in making what we see. The computer games we play and Internet sites we visit are developed by programmers. Rather than only being users of media, we can teach our children to be active participants in the process!

A fun and easy way to start is by creating a multimedia scrapbook about your family. Involve everyone in collecting or taking photos, researching pictures, writing captions, and even recording favorite memories and songs. Each family member can contribute different skills. Some kids might enjoy cropping photos; others might want to design page layouts, write journal entries, or record voice-overs. Experiencing the creative media process and seeing the finished product help kids appreciate the fruits of media.

TARGET MOMENT

Check out travel films or special-interest slide shows available at your local libraries or community centers. Plan an evening out watching these travel films with the whole family, then end the media event with a special ice-cream treat as you chat about all you learned!

Have family members each list five topics they would like to know more about. Choose one from each person's list to be the focus of recordings, documentaries, scrapbooks, and other family media projects.

key point

LOOK FOR WAYS TO CREATE FAMILY MEDIA.

For a more technical media project, consider making a documentary. Again, the family can brainstorm and decide on the focus of the film. Depending on your family's interests, you might prefer to make a Christian music video or fantasy film. The important thing is to work together, to commit to spending this time as a family, and to make the learning fun.

When your family wants to passively enjoy a movie or TV show, take advantage of TiVo or your VCR for your media "event." The advent of these technologies makes it possible to manage when and what we enjoy on the screen. Let each person choose a movie or show once a week to share with the family. Then grab cuddly blankets, pop up the popcorn, and make your own family media event inviting, relaxing, and filled with quality time shared by your family!

TIPS FOR 'TWEENS

Enroll your 'tween in a Web site design class. She can lead the development of a family Web site, where you can share photos and news with friends and long-distance family members!

key point

MAKE MEDIA EXCITING.

Check out Christian media alternatives.

As long as media influences our children, why not direct them to songs about following God and books and movies that help them strengthen their faith?

Christian media comes in exciting forms.

To explore what Christian media has to offer, you just need to know where to look. For starters, find out if there is a Christian bookstore in your area. These stores typically carry everything from videos for young children to inspirational books and CDs for older kids and adults.

You may wonder what defines media as Christian or "inspirational." Christian movies and music aren't necessarily about the life of Christ, but most include positive portrayals of characters and truths with Christ-like values. These movies and songs affirm rather than dispute the values we're teaching our kids.

If you don't have a local Christian bookstore, many booksellers have Christian sections and can order books or music they don't carry. Also, check out online Christian bookstores for a great multimedia selection of Christian products!

key point
PARENTAL OVERSIGHT IS STILL NECESSARY.

key point
CHRISTIAN MEDIA PUMPS UP FAITH.

Sales of contemporary Christian music were $747 million in 2000. Add movies and books, and the total is close to $3 billion!

TARGET MOMENT
In addition to movies and CDs, check out Christian Web sites and online Bibles with your child. There are interactive puzzles to help you learn Scripture and activity and coloring pages to run off on your printer.

Simply because a film or book is Christian doesn't mean it's appropriate for a child of any age. Many Christian authors deal with mature themes, like abstinence or recovering from sexual abuse, and are targeted at an older audience. For guidance on age-appropriate books and movies, check out www.commonsensemedia.org. It's also worth surfing to www.pluggedinonline.com, a Focus on the Family resource that provides in-depth and sensible movie reviews from a Christian perspective.

HERE ARE SEVERAL EXCITING SITES FOR CHRISTIAN MULTI-MEDIA RESOURCES!

- **www.heavenandearthonline.com**
  (Bibles, books, music, kids videos, and more for all ages)

- **www.christianityfreebies.com**
  (FREE goodies, including books, videos, gifts, kids' music CDs, and loads more for all ages)

- **www.ministryandmedia.com**
  (Bibles, books, reviews, music, news, and more for 'tweens and teens)

- **www.christianbook.com**
  (Bibles, books, reviews, music, gifts, videos, DVDs, and more for all ages)

TIPS FOR TODDLERS

Parents of toddlers and preschoolers can share Christian media with their kids from the very beginning. Explore these wonderful resources:

- **Playtime Devotions, by Christine Harder Tangvald (Standard Publishing, 2002)**

- **My Good-Night Bible, by Susan L. Lingo (Standard Publishing, 1999)**

- **Beginner's Bible for Toddlers, by Carolyn Nabors Baker and Danny Brooks Dalby (Tommy Nelson, 1995)**

- **Veggie Tales (Big Idea Productions)**

Many Web sites provide kids with true stories, advice, music tidbits, and trivia on hot topics like self-esteem and defending your faith. Whether it's lively CDs, comical cartoons, inspirational books, or even the Bible on CD, there's something for everyone in Christian media products and resources!

Christian media alternatives can help our witness.

So much of the "popular" media tells our kids that happiness is based on having things, that being cool is paramount, and that joy comes from living in the moment. It's powerful for our kids to hear messages that counter these from adults who aren't raising them. These media messages reinforce and validate what we're teaching at home.

key point
CHRISTIAN MEDIA EXCITES AND TEACHES.

key point
GOD USES MEDIA TO WITNESS.

Your older child may enjoy recording her favorite verses to share with friends. Record the verses below, then decorate tape or CD cases to hold the recordings. Encourage your child to present these special gifts to friends and family members.

- **John 3:16**
- **Romans 6:23**
- **Ephesians 2:8-10**

Sharing your faith and what Jesus has done for you is called "witnessing." It's good for kids to hear what their own parents think about Jesus and His influence in their lives. After watching a Christian movie or Bible-based show, chat with your child about the power Jesus has in your own life.

After our kids discover Christian media that excites them, they'll want to share it with others. Depending on their ages, this moment can be both challenging and pivotal in their spiritual growth. When a friend asks why they like the book *How to Live Like a King's Kid* (Bridge-Logos, 2000), our kids can convey their beliefs to others and define their faith! Encourage your child to create a short commercial for God or a statement expressing his faith now to help him express his beliefs with conviction and confidence later.

When kids share their faith, God often uses them to minister to others. Because kids don't know when God will use them, we should teach them to "clothe [themselves] with compassion, kindness, humility, gentleness and patience" as they seek to share their faith (Colossians 3:12)!

BIG BIBLE POINT

Read 2 Timothy 4:2 with your child. Then discuss the following questions:

- *How does listening to uplifting, Christian music help us be ready to tell others about Jesus?*
- *How does hearing God's Word spoken on a CD or Bible on tape help us learn the Word?*
- *How can watching biblical movies or movies with Christian values strengthen our own faith? help us tell others about our faith?*

Make a cool video of what family members have to say about Jesus, forgiveness, and what their favorite Scripture verses are. Record each family member's witness and verses, then make copies to play anytime family members need a bit of encouragement or a powerful reminder of your family's conviction of faith!

When kids demonstrate these attributes, others see the impact God has had in their lives. If they encounter skeptics who misunderstand the faith, kids can be ready to share their favorite Christian music or movies. It's also a good time for kids to explain that Christ died on the cross to forgive our sins and that the gift of salvation is open to all who receive it. When our kids hear awesome Christian songs, watch inspiring movies, or even listen to Scripture on CD, they become open to God's invitation to witness to others and share the life-changing Good News!

More Resources

BOOKS
for parents
- Kurt Bruner and Jim Weidmann, **Family Nights Package** (Focus on the Family).
- Gloria Degaetano and Kathleen Bander, **Screen Smarts: A Family Guide to Media Literacy** (Houghton Mifflin, 1996).
- Jane M. Healy, **Endangered Minds: Why Children Don't Think and What We Can Do About It** (Simon & Schuster, 1999).
- Jacqueline Lederman, **Joy Ride!** (Tyndale House, 2000). Exciting games for car trips.
- Bob Smithouser, **Movie Nights: 25 Movies to Spark Spiritual Discussions With Your Teen** (Tyndale House, 2002).
- Frank York and Jan LaRue, **Protecting Your Child in an X-Rated World** (Focus on the Family, 2002).

MAGAZINES
for parents
- **Christian Parenting Today** (Christianity Today, Inc.). Christian counsel, ideas, and articles for parents.
- **Plugged In** (Focus on the Family). Entertainment reviews, stories, and opinions from a Christian perspective.

for kids
- **Babybug**, for six months–two years; **Ladybug,** for kids two to six; **Spider,** ages six to nine (Cricket Magazine Group).
- **Kids Discover** (Kids Discover).
- **National Geographic Kids** (National Geographic Society).
- **Ranger Rick** (National Wildlife Federation).

MUSIC

for younger kids

- *102 Bible Songs* (Twin Sisters Productions).
- *This Little Light of Mine,* by Raffi Stacey Schuett (Random House, 2004). Book and CD set.
- *Wee Sing Bible Songs,* by Pamela Conn Beall (Penguin Putnam, 2002). Book and CD set.

for older kids

- *All Things New,* by Steven Curtis Chapman (Sparrow, 2004).
- *The Answer to the Question,* by Tree63 (Inpop, 2004).
- *Casting Crowns,* by Casting Crowns (Beach Street/Reunion, 2003).
- *Healing Rain,* by Michael W. Smith (Reunion, 2004).
- *Undone,* by MercyMe (INO Records, 2004).

DVDS/VIDEOS

- *Buzby the Misbehaving Bee* (Thomas Nelson).
- **McGee and Me Series** (Tyndale House).
- **Veggie Tales Series** (Big Idea Productions).

WEB SITES

for younger kids

- **www.christiananswers.net/kids/home.html.** Coloring pages and more for kids of all ages.
- **www.funbrain.com.** Interactive games and activities.
- **www.kidssundayschool.com.** Kids Sunday School Place.

for older kids

- **www.yahooligans.yahoo.com/parents.** Tips on safe surfing.
- **www.biblegateway.com.** Search the Bible online.
- **www.christianbook.com.** Christian videos, books, music, and more.
- **www.focusonyourchild.com.** Tips from Focus on the Family.

for 'tweens and teens

- **www.christiananswers.net.** Fun and educational activities.
- **kids.msfc.nasa.gov.** Games, activities, and information for kids from NASA.
- **www.christianyouthweb.com.** Games, missions, and current events.
- **www.websmartkids.com/arts.htm.** Fun and learning for 'tweens.
- **www.youthfire.com.** Chat, entertainment reviews, and articles.

Subpoint Index

Chapter 3: Media and Its Impact   56

Chapter 4: Mediating Choices   76